T0208814

HOW TO PLAN YOUR WAY TO SUCCESS

PERSONAL | FINANCIAL | REAL ESTATE | BUSINESS | HEALTH AND WELLNESS

FENOL E. | PREA ZWARYCH

HOW TO PLAN YOUR WAY TO SUCCESS
Personal | Financial | Real Estate | Business | Health and Wellness

iUniverse books may be ordered through booksellers or by contacting:

iUniverse
1663 Liberty Drive
Bloomington, IN 47403
www.iuniverse.com
1-800-Authors (1-800-288-4677)

Because of the dynamic nature of the Internet, any web addresses or links contained in this book may have changed since publication and may no longer be valid. The views expressed in this work are solely those of the author and do not necessarily reflect the views of the publisher, and the publisher hereby disclaims any responsibility for them.

Any people depicted in stock imagery provided by Thinkstock are models, and such images are being used for illustrative purposes only. Certain stock imagery © Thinkstock.

ISBN: 978-1-5320-1785-8 (sc)
ISBN: 978-1-5320-1787-2 (hc)
ISBN: 978-1-5320-1786-5 (e)

Print information available on the last page.

iUniverse rev. date: 04/18/2017

Success doesn't happen by itself.
Success must be planned.

CONTENTS

Wherever you are now in life is not your final destination. Whatever you are going through or whatever challenges you are facing at the moment are not meant to be in your life forever. With courage, perseverance, and constant action steps toward your goals and what you desire most in life, you will open new doors for yourself and create your new reality.

You were born to succeed and born to win.

INTRODUCTION

Success is something people always talk about. Success means different things to different people. Maybe for you it means having a lot of money, living a healthier and more joyful lifestyle, being able to travel the world, creating a wonderful family, or having a great career. What do you envision for your life? Whatever success means to you, living a successful life with purpose and direction requires planning, goal setting, and taking action.

There are so many people who have goals and dreams, but they have no idea how to achieve them. Others struggle financially, or have great business ideas, but they don't have the skills, knowledge, education, or proper guidance to improve their finances or to get their business ideas off the ground.

How to Plan Your Way to Success explains what you need to know and the steps you need to take NOW to reach your targeted goals. This essential guidebook and planner will also enable you to finally implement your ideas and launch that new business, to expand your finances, and to fully optimize your health and wellness.

Use this book to thoroughly identify, plan, and take action on your personal, financial, business, and health and wellness goals.

****

Take the time to fill out all the sections of this book. You can read through each chapter or the whole book, and then go back and answer the questions for your life, or you can fill out the answers in the book as you read it.

****

PLAN
YOUR LIFE

Plan Your Life

LIFE PLANNING - PART 1: WHERE ARE YOU GOING IN YOUR LIFE?

Goal-setting helps you move forward in every area of life whether it's in your personal, financial, business, professional, health, social, or spiritual life. Goals are mandatory in order to overcome living an aimless life with no direction or purpose. It is important to have your goals at the forefront of your mind at all times because they will determine what decisions you do or don't make throughout each day, week, month, and year, including what you spend your time doing and who you spend your time with. Furthermore, goals require action. Use the following pages to plan your goals and the action steps required to see your goals fulfilled.

Before you start setting specific goals, take some time to reflect on your life and what you really want to accomplish, including what you want your ideal dream life to be like.

What I desire to achieve and accomplish in my life:

_____
_____
_____
_____
_____

Activity #1: How You See Your Life

Current Date: _____

1) How do I want my life to be in...?

5 years: _____

10 years: _____

20 years: _____

2) If I didn't change anything about what I'm doing now, where could that lead me to be in...?

5 years: _____

10 years: _____

20 years: _____

If I am not satisfied with those answers, what can I do to change now so I can be on the path I want to be?

_____

_____

_____

_____

Ask yourself these questions:

1. What is needed to improve my current situation? _____

_____

_____

2. What services can I offer to the world? _____

_____

_____

3. What steps can I take today to work toward this? _____

_____

_____

4. Where can I go/Whom can I contact to get help with this?

_____

_____

Activity #2: Make a Vision Board

- A Vision Board is a valuable tool and motivator to have to give you a visual of where you are going in your life, including what you are striving for and where you desire to be.

- Make a Vision Board that shows exactly what you envision your future life to be like, in 5, 10, and 20 years. Print out images or words from the internet, and cut them out from magazines or anywhere, and post them on Bristol board, cardboard, presentation board, or a bulletin board. Put it up in your house where you can see it all the time. You may make different boards for each time period or different areas of your life.

- Also, keep visuals on your electronic devices that inspire you so that you can look at them easily.

Images and Words to include on my Vision Board:

_____

_____

_____

_____

Activity #3: Make Your Life Vision Statement

Here is a summary of my Life Vision:

In _____ **years, I will be** _____ , _____

_____ , **and** _____ .

I will have _____ , _____ , **and**

_____ .

With the majority of my time, I will _____ ,

_____ , **and** _____ .

In my spare time, I will _____ ,

_____ , **and** _____ .

I will create $ _____ **with this dream.**

Write a 1-2 line statement that briefly but thoroughly sums up your Vision. This is the statement that you can rehearse in your head and post up on your wall, mirror, fridge, car, to keep you focused and to keep you going.

_____

_____

_____

LIFE PLANNING - PART 2: SETTING YOUR GOALS

GOAL-SETTING STRATEGIES

1. **Make sure your goals follow the SMART goal rubric:**
   - **Specific** – what *exactly* is the goal? The What? Why? And How?
   - **Measurable** – as in *not* vague; you can know exactly when you've achieved it (E.g., "My goal is to have more money" is too vague. A better goal is "in 3 years, I want to have a regular income of $5000/month." This is much

more measurable because you can easily know when you've attained it.

- o We add: **Money-Generating** – how will this goal enable you to generate an income from it? If the original intention is not to live off the income from this goal, think of ways it can generate money anyway.
- **Attainable** – something you can actually do.
- **Realistic** – also stands for **Relevant** or **Results-based** (goals based on results of a task, not just doing the task).
- **Time-based** – give yourself a reasonable deadline to strive for. If you need to extend it later, it's fine as long as you are making considerable progress on it now.
  -Estimate how long it will take you to achieve each goal.

2. **Have specific, well-defined goals written down** so you can see them tangibly in front of you. If you don't have strong, specific goals, you'll just do anything that comes along, and you won't get anywhere.

3. **Don't let your goals be too broad** because then it is more difficult to pinpoint when you have achieved them.

4. **If you have many dreams,** it is better to focus all your energy on pursuing one dream at a time. We recommend first pursuing the dream that will improve your life the most and allow you to provide for your family.

5. **Narrow your focus** to one or two goals at a time; this enables you to make more progress on them because then all your energy goes into those goals alone.

6. **Break your goals down into smaller tasks** that you can easily visualize yourself accomplishing in short time-frames.

7. **When setting your goals, think backwards:** What do you want to have accomplished by the end of the month? Write down what you have to accomplish each week to get there, and then write down what you have to accomplish each day to reach your weekly goals.

8. **Set "Performance" goals vs. "Outcome" goals,** meaning: Set your goal to measure your own performance, not the outcome of an activity. For example, your goal can be to play the best in your sport that you can, but you still cannot guarantee that you will win the gold medal (the "outcome"). You can only do your personal best.

NOW SET YOUR GOALS

Long-Term Goals: Answer the following questions to determine your long-term goals. Your long-term goals are the goals you can accomplish within the next 5, 10, or 20 years.

1. **To live my ideal life, what major things will I have to accomplish?**

   _____

   _____

   _____

   _____

2. **Which of those things can I start pursuing first? Second? Third?**

   _____

   _____

   _____

3. **Set these as my long-term goals. When do I want to have each of those long-term goals accomplished by?**

_____

_____

_____

_____

4. **List of things I will need or will need to do in order to accomplish these long-term goals:**

_____

_____

_____

_____

Short-Term Goals

Short-term goals are all the smaller steps in between each long-term goals that are needed to reach the long-term goals. Short-term goals should be:

- Able to be achieved within 1 year.
- Designed to bring you closer to your long-term goals.
- All you need to do over the next 1 month, 6 months, and 12 months toward your long-term goals.
- Small enough so you can feel as though you are achieving things and making progress.
- Broken down into monthly, weekly, and daily tasks so you can have a clear idea of what you need to do.

As you accomplish more goals and tasks, they will inevitably lead to more follow-up tasks that you will have to add to your list of things to do as well. Prioritize them within your master task list.

5. **What Short-term goals (6 months to 1 year) do I need to accomplish that will help me achieve my Long-term goals?**

_____

_____

_____

_____

6. **What I will do now/today/this week, in order to start working toward these goals:**

_____

_____

_____

_____

Activity # 4: GOAL FLOWCHART

Work backwards from your Ultimate Goal to identify the steps that are needed to get there.

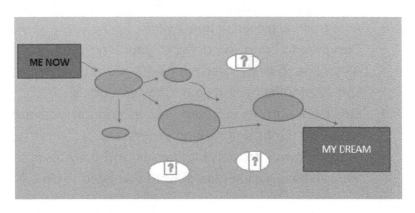

- On a separate piece of paper or on a fresh page in a notebook, draw a rectangle on the farthest left side of the page with the words "Me Now" in it. On the farthest right side of the page, draw a rectangle, and write inside it your Ultimate Goal ("My Dream").

- In between the rectangles, draw large circles representing the major goals you will need to accomplish in order to achieve your Ultimate Goal. Draw arrows coming from those circles stating the tasks you will need to do to achieve those major goals.

- Continue for as many tasks that you can think of showing each step you would need to do to achieve the goal.

- For each step you have to do, ask yourself, is this a task I could do tomorrow?

- If not, then ask yourself, "What would I have to do before I can do that step?"

- Add that answer to the end of an arrow. Then ask if you can do *that* new step tomorrow. If still not, then record what you would need in order to do it.

- Keep working backwards until you reach the action steps you can actually do *today* (or this week).

- Some steps may lead to a question mark on the left side because you actually don't know what you need to do to accomplish that step. In that case, you will have to complete some other steps around it to discover what that blank spot should be.

- Ask yourself what barriers there are between accomplishing any of these steps and what must be done to overcome them.

- For example, maybe you have to save money or make a significant investment in order to accomplish one of the tasks.
- Whatever resources you need, ask around for them. Don't be afraid. This is your life. You are the only one who can take the necessary steps to accomplish your dreams.

Activity # 5: 1 YEAR AND 2 YEAR GOAL PLANNING CHART

On a large piece of paper, record in the box for that month what you want to have accomplished by each month for the next 2 years. This may include any deadlines for things you have to submit or prepare for. It will include things you have to plan well in advance, such as what you will do by each month to meet your deadline. You can use these boxes to record important deadlines, or create a large scale planner to have more space to write in more detail what you have to do each month.

Year	JAN	FEB	MAR	APR	MAY	JUNE	JULY	AUG	SEPT	OCT	NOV	DEC
20__												
20__												

Activity # 6: ANTICIPATE AND OVERCOME OBSTACLES & CHALLENGES

1. **What in my life now may be preventing me from accomplishing my Long-term or Short-term goals?**

_____

_____

_____

_____

2. **What can I do to overcome these obstacles? Set these as goals.**

_____

_____

_____

_____

3. **What are some potential future challenges that may arise?**

_____

_____

_____

_____

4. **What can I do now or in advance to prepare me to overcome or avoid any future challenges?**

_____

_____

_____

_____

_____

TO DO LIST:

_____

_____

_____

_____

_____

_____

_____

_____

HOW TO PRIORITIZE YOUR GOALS

In order to help you determine which goals to pursue first, ask yourself the following questions:

1. Which goal(s) do I think about the most?
2. Which goals make me excited when I think about them?
3. Which goals do I have a sense of urgency to start working on right away?
4. What accomplishments would make me feel the most proud of myself?
5. Which accomplishments can I take with me forever? Which accomplishments would seem the most permanent to me? Is this important to me?
6. Ten years from now, how important will the goal be to me?
7. Which goals are fully within my control and not too dependent on other people or circumstances?
8. Is this goal something other people think I should do or something I want to do?
9. If I could do absolutely anything relating to accomplishing my goals, without any obstacles in my way, what would it be?

TIPS FOR WHEN YOU HAVE MANY TASKS TO DO AT ONCE

1. **Group like-tasks together**; avoid spreading yourself too thin by trying to multi-task too much.
2. **Do the most important tasks first**, and don't switch tasks often or do anything else non-related to your action plan goals. Remove distractions.

3. **For tasks that must be done at the same time or that have the same deadline, set a time by which you will accomplish the first task,** and then move to the next one. Set a timer or alarm if necessary.

15 GENERAL HABIT-RELATED TIPS TO HELP YOU ACCOMPLISH YOUR GOALS

1. **Once you know what your main goals are, cut away every other task and activity that does not align with them** so that you can devote all your attention and energy to accomplishing those goals. You must be willing to temporarily let certain activities go so better things can come.
2. **Every night, make your To-Do list for the next day.** When you wake-up, you know immediately what you have to do that day and don't have to waste any time planning your To-Do list the day of. Check off your list as you complete each task, and keep your list handy so you can see your progress throughout the day.
3. **Take action every day, and don't procrastinate.**
4. **Plan ahead, and persevere no matter what.**
5. **Prioritize your tasks constantly, and be flexible,** especially as unexpected situations arise.
6. **Work during your peak energy time,** and create the environment needed for you to be the most productive.
7. **Work in smaller periods of time instead of long batches of time.** Take necessary breaks. Your body can focus better in small batches of time.
8. **Make full use of the 24 hours in a day,** especially because your goals are time-based. If in 1-2 years you

want to be somewhere, then every moment counts now so that you don't waste time now and then have to do double the amount of work next year. With steady work early on in the journey, you may even be able to accomplish more goals earlier than planned.

9. **Block out time** for yourself, and block out time for others (set appointments).

10. **Expect discomfort.** Times will come when there will be more enjoyable things to do than to be working on your goal, but you must have the willpower to withstand the temptation to "just hang out with friends", for example, or to accept every invitation to do something else.

11. **Stay organized.** Keep an organized work space and file system within an organized work environment.

12. **Be consistent** with your routine and good work habits.

13. **Do what you do best, and delegate the rest.** Don't get caught in tasks that will slow you down from the main work you must do. If someone else can do it and it will help free up your time to get other tasks done, or they are more experienced at it than you and therefore the task will be done better, then let someone else do it. You may have to compensate someone monetarily for helping you out.

14. **Review what you've done each week, and measure your progress.** Reward yourself for what you have accomplished, and celebrate milestones.

15. **Keep track of your progress.** Keep a notebook to record everything you do each day. That way you can see what you did toward your goals each day and maybe where you didn't use your time the most wisely, indicating where you can improve your use of time in the future.

5 PERSONAL DEVELOPMENT TIPS THAT WILL HELP YOU ACCOMPLISH YOUR GOALS

1. **Affirm your success**; speak it out loud in present tense. Maintain the right mindset.
2. **Recognize self-defeating habits, and replace them** with positive habits.
3. **Eat healthy and exercise** so your body can feel good, strong, and energized. Having a healthy body helps you to focus on accomplishing your work instead of being sick in bed or having to take days off to restore your body. Maintain a healthy lifestyle so you have the health and strength to pursue your dreams and goals.
4. **Ignore negative attitudes and words** from others about what you're doing.
5. **Maintain a strong support system from your friends and family**; keep the ones close who encourage and support you and who respect your time to work. Avoid those who use up all your time unnecessarily.

Review the Outcome After Having Achieved a Goal

When you have achieved a goal, review the rest of your goal plans by considering the following:

- If you achieved the goal too easily, make your next goal harder.
- If the goal took a discouraging length of time to achieve, make the next goal a little easier.
- If you learned something that would lead you to change other goals, do so.
- If you noticed a lack in your skills despite achieving the goal, decide whether to work on improving your skills in that certain area.

Use any lessons learned to influence your other goal setting. Adjust your goals to reflect your new knowledge and experience.

Lessons Learned from Achieving a Goal:

_____

_____

_____

_____

_____

Identify any unexpected obstacles that arose while working toward that goal and how you overcame them:

_____

_____

_____

_____

_____

PLAN YOUR BUSINESS

Plan Your Business

Anyone can start a business, no matter what age or what background. To create a business is to create a source of income that you are in control of, which is the best way to go. With a business, you have the potential to create unlimited income, with no limits to your earning potential set in place by employers. You could start a simple side business or a large corporation. It could be an internet-based business, a product-based business, or a service-based business. Or you could develop and build an invention that helps people with something they need. There is no limit to the number of businesses you can start. Whatever you do, you need to think about and plan out every detail of your business ideas, as much as you can in advance, in order to be as prepared as possible for a successful venture. Use the following questions to get you started thinking about and planning your businesses in detail:

BUSINESS PLANNER

BUSINESS IDEA #1
Title: _____
    1. Describe my business idea:

_____
_____
_____
_____

2. What is the purpose of this business? _____

   _____

   _____

3. What is the problem this business is going to solve?

   _____

   _____

4. How will my idea help people and serve the world?

   _____

   _____

5. How is it different or better than other similar products/ services? _____

   _____

   _____

6. Whatever my product/service is providing to others, how are people currently getting that product/ service? _____

   _____

   _____

7. Who are my competitors? _____

   _____

   _____

8. Do I want to offer this product/service because I like it or need it or because other people will like it or need it? _____

   _____

   _____

9. How will I get the materials for my product/service?

   _____

   _____

10. Who is my Target Market? Who will buy the product/
    service? _____

    _____

    _____

11. Why do I want to target this clientele over another type
    of clientele? _____

    _____

12. How much of the market will my product/service attract
    (e.g., 5% of the population or 90%)? _____

    _____

13. How will I promote this product/service? _____

    _____

    _____

14. What kind of entity will I form and why? Sole
    proprietorship, General partnership, or Corporation?

    _____

    _____

15. Will I have business partners? If so, who are they?

    _____

    _____

16. Who will be on my team that I can trust and talk to?

    _____

    _____

17. How can I make my business run by itself online?

_____

_____

18. Can I blend this idea with another idea that already exists? _____

_____

_____

Test Your Idea

Before establishing your entire business, you will want to know that it has a chance of being very successful and that it is actually in demand by the market. Ask yourself:

19. How can I make a sample of my product/service and start providing it to people to begin gaining valuable feedback?

_____

_____

_____

20. Feedback from others on your product/service:

_____

_____

_____

_____

21. Notes on ways my idea can be improved:

_____

_____

_____

_____

Plan for Start-Up Costs

Depending on how you register your business and what is needed for your particular business, it could be between $5000-$10,000 to start up. Here is a list of typical new business expenses to plan for:

- Logo, Business Cards, Website, Flyers, Promotion
- Lawyer, Accountant
- Legal fees (registration/incorporation, copyright/ trademark), Bank account fees
- Equipment, Office Supplies
- Business Clothes, Professional Photos
- Computer software (to keep track of clients and accounting software)
- Office Space/Building/Property, Business phone number

22. Make a list of all the things you will need in place to start officially and professionally operating your business. List the costs associated with each item. (You may have to do some research.)

_____

_____

_____

_____

_____

_____

TIPS:
- See if there are any items or areas you can make do without for now until your business starts generating regular income.

- See what resources you can acquire at a discounted rate.
- Be creative and resourceful.

23. How will I obtain the funds to finance this idea?

_____

_____

_____

_____

<u>OVERCOMING OBSTACLES</u>

24. Pros and Cons of this idea:

_____

_____

_____

_____

25. What obstacles may arise that might try to prevent me from pursuing this idea?

_____

_____

_____

_____

26. What can I do to anticipate, prepare for, and overcome these obstacles?

_____

_____

_____

_____

27. What are some potential future challenges that may arise?

_____

_____

_____

_____

28. What can I do now or in advance to prepare to overcome or avoid any future challenges?

_____

_____

_____

_____

START TAKING ACTION

29. Things I need to figure out before moving forward with this idea:

_____

_____

_____

_____

30. When do I want to have this idea started by?

_____

_____

31. What can I do this week to make progress on this business idea?

_____

_____

_____

32. What can I do this month to make progress on this business idea?

_____

_____

_____

_____

33. What do I want to have accomplished by the end of this year?

_____

_____

_____

_____

34. What will this business look like when running successfully?

_____

_____

_____

_____

35. Milestones for this business idea:

_____ Date achieved: _____

_____ Date achieved: _____

_____ Date achieved: _____

_____ Date achieved: _____

_____ Date achieved: _____

36. Make a Vision Board to create a physical visual of this idea. You can use presentation board, Bristol board, or a bulletin board. Gather pictures and words printed from the internet or cut outs from magazines that

show your ultimate dream goal for your business in its most successful state that you can imagine. Display your Vision Board in a visible place in your home so you can always see it and be motivated and inspired by it.

Keep a version on your electronic devices as well so you can quickly access it for motivational breaks, even if it is just a folder with all your gathered pictures that you can scroll through.

In fact, keep inspiring words and pictures in all areas of your living and work space so you are constantly surrounded by visuals of your dreams and goals. Images and Words to include on my Vision Board:

_____

_____

_____

_____

TO DO LIST:

_____

_____

_____

_____

_____

_____

_____

Identify and differentiate between your Urgent and Important tasks versus your Not Urgent tasks relating to this Idea: _____

_____

_____

_____

_____

_____

_____

_____

What I did this week to work on this project:

_____

_____

_____

_____

_____

_____

Find your Mastermind Group and Like-Minded Community:

- Get a mentor or coach who will push you and challenge you.
- Get involved in circles of business people and entrepreneurs because you can benefit from their experience and knowledge.
- Join groups and communities of people in the same field; you need a support network, not just you going on the journey alone.

- It is beneficial to have a close team of people you can trust and talk to in depth and who will keep you motivated and encouraged.
- A wider community of people is beneficial to share with and to learn from their mistakes and challenges.

Who are my mentors/coaches? _____

_____

What online or physical communities or meet-up groups can I join that would be beneficial to my business idea?

_____

_____

_____

_____

Once you have developed your ideas enough and are ready to move forward, make a formal Business Plan to summarize the planning and brainstorming you have just done.

As you get other business ideas, repeat all of these valuable planning steps for each idea.

_____

_____

_____

_____

_____

_____

_____

_____

_____

BUSINESS PLAN OUTLINE

1. **Cover Page** – State your company name, title of the document ("Business Plan"), date, and business contact information including owner's name, business address, phone number, and website.

    _____

    _____

    _____

    _____

2. **Table of Contents** – Outlines the location of the specific sections in the business plan.

3. **Statement of Purpose** – Describe the business and the products or services you plan to provide. Describe how the business is structured and the total amount of funding needed to start the business.

    _____

    _____

    _____

    _____

    _____

    _____

4. **Executive Summary** – Summarizes the business plan with the key points from each of the other sections. It should interesting enough to intrigue readers, who may be potential investors, to keep reading your entire business plan. The Executive Summary should not be more than two pages long, and should be written last,

only once all the other questions in the Main Body are answered.

_____

_____

_____

_____

_____

_____

Main Body

5. **Historical Account of your Business or Business Idea** – Describe how you came up with this business idea and how you are qualified to execute it.

_____

_____

_____

_____

_____

_____

6. **Goals and Objectives** – Describe your short-term (1 year) and long-term (5-10 year) goals for your business and how you realistically see your business in the future.

_____

_____

_____

_____

_____

_____

7. **Your Products or Services** – Clearly outline the details of your products and services and the value of what you will be offering to customers. Describe what makes your products or services unique.

_____

_____

_____

_____

_____

_____

_____

_____

_____

8. **Location** – State your desired location where of your business will operate. Describe the demographics and statistics of this area. For example, if you are starting a trendy women's clothing store, you could find statistics on how many females between the ages of 18-40 are living in the area where you plan to locate your business.

_____

_____

_____

_____

_____

_____

_____

_____

9. **Management/Ownership** – Describe the management team and the relevant experience and benefits each

member brings to the business. Also describe the role each person will play in the business and the responsibilities they will have.

_____

_____

_____

_____

_____

_____

_____

_____

_____

_____

10. **Marketing Plan** – Describe your target market in detail and the strategies you will use to make sure they know about your product or service. Also outline your strategies for pricing, and advertising and promotion.

_____

_____

_____

_____

_____

_____

_____

_____

_____

11. **Competitive Analysis** - Identify your competition and analyze your competition's strengths and weaknesses.

Determine incentives that will encourage customers to choose your business over the competition.

_____

_____

_____

_____

_____

_____

_____

_____

_____

_____

12. **Current and Projected Financial Statements:**
    a. Financial Statements – Work out the numbers to see if your business makes sense financially. Investors will want to see numbers that show your business will grow. Create a sales forecast, cash flow statement, income statement, balance sheet, and expense budget. The numbers will come from your best estimates based on past data.

_____

_____

_____

_____

_____

_____

_____

_____

_____

_____

_____

b. Identify Risks – Identify the risks and challenges your business faces and the strategies you can use to deal with them.

_____

_____

_____

_____

_____

_____

_____

_____

_____

c. Investments Needed – Identify the amount of money needed to start your business and how the funds will be allotted across the various expenses. Determine when you plan to pay back any money borrowed.

_____

_____

_____

_____

_____

_____

_____

_____

_____

_____

13. **Appendix** – Include factual information to support the previous sections of the business plan, such as photos of your product, resumes of management and owners, results of market research, legal documents, and spreadsheets showing financial details. You can add or remove documents from the Appendix depending on who will be reading the business plan.

Documents to include in the Appendix:

_____

_____

_____

_____

_____

_____

_____

_____

_____

_____

PLAN YOUR FINANCES

Plan Your Finances

THE HISTORY OF MONEY AND HOW THE BANKING SYSTEM WORKS

The only real money that ever existed in the world is gold or silver. Many things, such as shells, beads, and livestock, and now most recently plastic and paper, have been used as currency. Currency is money that is backed by nothing but air, which means it is only valuable because people believe that it is valuable. The actual paper dollar has no real value in it. Money used to be backed by gold, but in 1971, President Nixon removed money from the gold standard, meaning it is no longer backed by gold; it's actually just paper, a form of currency.

When our paper money, which is called "fiat (fake) currency," loses its value, gold and silver still retain their real value and are accepted anywhere in the world as real money.

History shows that sooner or later, the manmade fiat money goes out of value due to governments borrowing too much money and banks printing too much money.

Banks are private entities owned by some of the richest families in the world. They are just businesses, and like most businesses, they are mainly interested in their own profit. Banks make their profit by charging interest. For banks, customers' debt = money because the more loans they give, the more money they make back from interest. When the banks and the government print money, it devalues your savings causing inflation, which means currency starts to have less value over time. As a result, you have to work harder to make less.

One example of your money having less value now is 20 years ago, you used to buy groceries for $35, but now you need to pay $100 for same amount of food. Inflation is silently eating up those who "save money" because the value of your $100 is going down, down, down with time.

So what do you do about it?
You need not to be caught in the system.

To protect yourself from inflation and losing your life savings due to currencies going out of value, you need to use your currency to acquire tangible assets, such as investment property, land, silver, and gold.

Placing your hard-earned money in someone else's hands to invest for you in the stock market or banks, where you have no control over it, is not the best way to grow your wealth. You should always maintain control over your money.

Banks, the place where you store your hard-earned currency, can ironically go bankrupt. With the economic challenges the world is experiencing these days, all that paper money you've worked so hard to save up, trading your time and life for, can be gone in a flash, but tangible assets like property and precious metals will always be valuable and can't go "out of business" like banks can. When the economy crashes, you lose your money, but when you have investment properties that you rent out and have gold and silver in your possession, you have something to fall back on.

Owning these types of tangible assets is what grows your wealth. Personal wealth is measured by the worth of the assets you own, not merely the amount of money in your bank account, which can disappear in a heartbeat. Also, these types of tangible assets are the types of investments that can protect you in the future, that can support you through retirement, and that you can pass down to your children, and your children's children.

HOW TO BUY GOLD AND SILVER

Gold and silver bars are better for investments than coins because they are easier to store, trade, and sell. You can store the physical bars in locked cases in different secretive places which you feel are safest. You order by weight from one ounce of .999 fine silver or .999 fine gold up to as many ounces you would like. Here are some of the most popular brands of silver and gold that you can purchase:

1. Sunshine (silver or gold)
2. Johnson Matthey (silver or gold)
3. Royal Canadian Mint Gold Wafer Bar
4. Credit Suisse Gold Wafer Bar

One trusted company that is easy to order online from (and to monitor the price per ounce since it fluctuates constantly) is Silver Gold Bull. For Canada the website is www.silvergoldbull.ca. If you live in the U.S. or anywhere else in the world, go to www. silvergoldbull.com.

SILVER & GOLD INVESTING PLAN

Use this chart to set up a plan to invest monthly in an order of silver or gold.

DATE	PRECIOUS METAL (Silver or Gold)	BRAND	OUNCES	PRICE

REAL ESTATE

In addition to owning silver and gold, use your currency to purchase investment property to increase your cash flow by renting to tenants. In order to increase your chances of success in real estate investing, seek expert advice from a real estate investing coach or a team of people who know about, and have experience in, investing in real estate.

The following is written by Eric Saumure, CPA, CA, President of Bytown Living:

It is imperative that, if you commit to invest in real estate, you must gather along your side a qualified team of individuals who will help guide you. An expert coach and mentor can really bridge that gap to help you learn and stay motivated toward your real estate goals. To help you determine your goals, here are some of the basic strategies to enable you to use real estate to generate active or passive income:

Active Income

- **Owner-occupied investment** – *A single family home for which you rent out the basement as a secondary suite. This allows you to save on your housing expenses considerably and maybe even pay your mortgage.*
- **Duplex/Triplex** – *A duplex (2 unit) or triplex (3 unit) building that can be rented out completely separately from your primary residence.*

Passive Income

- **Mortgage products** – *The passive investors invest money with an active real estate investor who owns the property. Mortgage investments are secured by the property in case of default and can be grouped with other investors as a syndicated mortgage.*
- **Syndicated ownership** – *The passive investor gets in touch with other passive investors and an active real estate investor to pool their money together to achieve some economies of scale in buying larger buildings (6+ residential units).*

All these options can earn you generous rates of returns. However, in some cases, you may be just starting your financial plan and may not be at a stage to be able to participate in these real estate investment strategies. However, there are numerous methods to still earn income from the real estate industry, without any significant financial commitment. One of the easiest methods is to "wholesale" properties. Wholesaling properties is basically doing the dirty work for real estate investors! Real estate investors are happy to pay you for doing the grunt work! You talk to real estate agents, visit properties and make offers on properties. Once you enter into an agreement for a property that you feel is a good potential investment, you can offer it up to real estate investors, in exchange for an assignment fee or finder's fee.

Pick the strategy you think works best with your other financial, life, and business goals. Evaluate the trade-offs of the value of your time and experience to determine if you would like to invest passively or actively.

***

Property Management

Success in real estate investing requires team work. Besides having a mentor or coach to keep you accountable, to guide you, and share a great wealth of knowledge to help you be successful, it is critical that you have the right management team in place to help you manage and take care of your investment properties.

Benefits of Hiring a Property Management Team

There are tremendous benefits when you outsource to an individual or a company to manage your property for you. Hiring a professional property management company is more economical and advantageous than many landlords and investors think. As the property owner, you get to enjoy the money coming in each month in the form of rent cheques from either long-term, short-term, or Airbnb tenants without much effort and without all the headaches that come with managing tenants and receiving those midnight and 3:00 a.m. phone calls about broken toilets, broken pipes, and electrical issues. More importantly, you get to have plenty of time to spend with your loved ones and travel the world as you wish. Also, by having a management team in place, you can focus your attention on buying more properties and investing in deals that will accelerate your real estate investing success process. Property management is designed to relieve you, the property owner, from the burden of the duties of property management so you can focus on what matters most to you.

Property Management Fees and Services

The fees a property management company charges on a monthly basis per door are usually around 6% to 8% of the monthly rent for long-term and short-term rentals and 12% to 20% for Airbnb rentals.

If you decide that you are going to manage the property yourself but don't want to spend time advertising for good quality tenants, and showing the property to potential tenants, which is all very consuming, you can hire a property manager to fill the vacant unit for a one-time fee of one month's rent.

Those fees are like grains of sand on a beach compared to how much cash flow the management company can help you bring in over time, especially if the person or company also owns investment properties and has a good amount of experience. These are the best kind of people to have on your team.

If your property isn't rented, or doesn't make any money that month or week, which is unlikely to happen under good management, the fees are not paid out to the property manager.

Property Management services include but are not limited to:

- Advertising
- Scheduling viewings
- Processing applications and screening
- Notifying of guest move-ins and move-outs
- Collecting rent
- Applying penalties and late fees
- Preparing and sending accounting statements monthly
- Communicating with tenants
- Managing services
- Inspecting units regularly
- Informing of any maintenance or tenant concerns
- Managing building operations, preventative maintenance, landscaping and snow removal
- Managing contractors
- Providing annual updates on your property and more

Like any business, the survival of your real estate business depends on good management and cash flow that your assets are creating. Your investment properties are supposed to bring money into your pockets, not take money out of your pockets. A great property management team will ensure you are getting the greatest possible return on your investment.

While they are doing what they do best, you have time to do what you do best.

***

See the Appendix for more detailed and thorough information and tips on Real Estate Investing, written by Bruce M. Firestone, PhD., Real Estate Investment Coach, Century 21 Explorer Realty Inc. broker, Ottawa Senators founder, @profbruce, www.brucemfirestone.com.

***

Action Steps I Can Take to Move Forward in My Real Estate Investing:

_____

_____

_____

_____

_____

My Investment Notes:

_____

_____

_____

_____

_____

_____

_____

_____

USING GOOD DEBT AND CONQUERING BAD DEBT

There are two types of debt – Bad debt and Good debt. Bad debt is money (or credit) spent on liabilities – things that lose value over time, starting from the day you buy them.

Good debt is money used for investing purposes – things that bring money back to you, such as real estate, businesses, and royalties on products like inventions, music, or books you produce.

You will likely use credit cards for both Good and Bad debt. Credit cards increase your borrowing capacity enabling you to start a business or acquire investment properties. Credit spent on these types of ventures would be considered Good debt because the income from the investments would pay off the credit cards. But be warned; you must be able to make significant payments on the credit cards because interest rates can cause the balances to quickly multiply out of control.

That being said, credit cards should not be used to purchase material things whose values go down. You should only use your credit card for investments which bring you the income you can use to pay off the card. According to Robert Kiyosaki, author of *Rich Dad, Poor Dad,* an asset is something that adds money into your pocket, while liabilities take money out of your pocket. Financially educated people use credit to acquire assets, while financially uneducated people use credit to buy liabilities – things whose value declines each passing day.

If you find yourself in deep credit card debt, you may be advised (by the financially uneducated) to cut up your credit card and never use it again, but don't do it! No matter what your situation is, do not cut up your credit card! First of all, closing a credit card does not look good on your credit score, and secondly, you can use that credit card to acquire income-generating investments! You simply need to exercise self-control and discipline to only use credit for things that put money into your pocket (assets), not things that take money out of your pocket forever (liabilities).

CREDIT SCORE

Having a good credit score will give you an advantage for your future endeavors over those with a bad credit score. You will need a good credit score in order to qualify for more credit, which you can use to invest in your business or real estate. Lenders check credit scores, so it is important to know where you stand. In Canada, the major credit bureaus are Equifax and TransUnion. Here is how they categorize the scores:

- Excellent Credit: 781-850
- Good Credit: 661-780
- Fair Credit: 601-660
- Poor Credit: 501-600
- Bad Credit: below 500

Where do you fit? One website you can use to quickly and easily see your credit score for free is www.creditkarma.ca. Research ways on how you can improve your credit score.

Strategies for Paying Off Bad Debt:

You want to get rid of all the bad debt so that you can free yourself to move forward on the things you really want to do in life that the bad debt may be holding you back from.

One strategy you can use to tackle the bad debt is to start by paying down the high interest debt first. Or, you can pay off the lower balances first since they will be paid down faster than larger balances. You will have to be sure to continue making minimum payments on the higher balances.

Make an action plan for what strategy you will use to pay off your bad debt by listing all your debt and recording the amount due for each, monthly. See which plan makes the most sense for you for what debts to get rid of first.

To help you pay down the credit cards, one way is to lower your expenses and cut back on spending, but often that is easier said than done. The other option is to get creative and find a way to increase your income.

See the appendix at the back of this book for strategies on how to minimize your expenses, overcome negative spending habits, and ways to increase your income.

MAKE A BUDGET AND KEEP TRACK OF YOUR MONEY USING THE FOLLOWING BUDGETING PLANNERS AND GUIDELINES.

Money Planning Activity #1

Calculate how much income you receive and how much you spend per month to see how much you have left over to put toward savings (for investing purposes), emergency fund (3-6 months of living expenses), and debt payments.

MONTHLY BUDGETING PLAN FOR _____

(Month/Year)

LIVING EXPENSES	
RENT/MORTGAGE PAYMENTS	$
CONDO FEE/PROPERTY TAXES	$
GROCERIES	$
CHILD CARE	$
CLOTHING	$
OTHER	$
SUBTOTAL	$
BILLS	
UTILITIES	$
HOME PHONE	$
CELL PHONE	$
CABLE/INTERNET	$
OTHER	$
SUBTOTAL	$

PERSONAL CARE	
GYM	$
COSMETICS	$
HAIR CARE	$
BODY CARE (SPA, TANNING)	$
HEALTH CARE (DENTAL & OTHER MEDICAL BILLS)	$
PRESCRIPTIONS	$
OTHER	$
SUBTOTAL	$

EDUCATION	
TUITION	$
BOOKS & SUPPLIES	$
SUBTOTAL	$

HOUSEKEEPING	
HOME REPAIRS/HOME SERVICES	$
HOME IMPROVEMENTS/DECOR	$
HOME OFFICE SUPPLIES	$
COMPUTER MAINTENANCE	$
LAUNDRY/DRY CLEANING	$
OTHER	$
SUBTOTAL	$
TRANSPORTATION	
PARKING	$
PARKING TICKETS	$
GAS	$
PUBLIC TRANSIT	$
TAXI/UBER	$
OTHER	$
SUBTOTAL	$

GENERAL EXPENSES	
CAR INSURANCE	$
HOME INSURANCE	$
LIFE INSURANCE	$
HEALTH INSURANCE	$

INVESTMENTS	$
TAXES	$
CAR LEASE PAYMENTS	$
CREDIT CARD PAYMENTS	$
STUDENT LOAN PAYMENTS	$
CHILDCARE	$
OTHER	$
SUBTOTAL	$

ENTERTAINMENT/LEISURE	
FOOD TAKE-OUT	$
RESTAURANTS	$
TRAVEL/VACATION	$
MOVIES	$
CONCERTS/PARTY TICKETS	$
ARCADE GAMES/VIDEO GAMES	$
BOOKS/MAGAZINES/NEWSPAPERS	$
NEW DEVICES	$
HOBBIES	$
OTHER	$
SUBTOTAL	$

GIVING	
DONATIONS	$
RANDOM GIVING	$
MONEY TRANSFER TO SUPPORT FAMILY/FRIENDS	$

OTHER	$
SUBTOTAL	$

EXTRA EXPENSES	
BANKING FEES	$
LEGAL/ACCOUNTING FEES	$
VETERINARIAN	$
PET FOOD/EXPENSES	$
GIFTS	$
OTHER	$
SUBTOTAL	$

Your Total Monthly Living Expenses (all money out)

= _____

Your Monthly Income – Your Total Monthly Expenses = Amount left over to divide between Savings, Emergency Fund, and Debt.

<u>Plan A</u>

_____ - _____ = _____

Monthly Income - Total Monthly Expenses = Divide b/w Savings, Emergency Fund & Debt

If your amount left over to divide between Savings, Emergency Fund, and Debt is not high enough to make an impact, you have to go back through the chart and find a way to reduce or cut out items AND find ways to increase your Monthly income!

Then try a Plan B and Plan C until you create a plan that works for you. Remember, you may have to make significant sacrifices with your time and comfort zone in order to work toward your financial goals.

Plan B

_____ - _____ = _____

Monthly Income - Total Monthly Expenses = Divide b/w Savings, Emergency Fund & Debt

Plan C

_____ - _____ = _____

Monthly Income - Total Monthly Expenses = Divide b/w Savings, Emergency Fund & Debt

SAVINGS	
SAVINGS	$
EMERGENCY FUND	$

DEBTS	
DEBT 1:	$
DEBT 2:	$
DEBT 3:	$

Money Planning Activity #2: DAILY EXPENSE LOG

Use this Daily Expense Log to record everything you spend every day so you can physically see your cash (or credit) going out. Most people spend more in a week or month than they realize. It is very easy not to notice those daily coffees or meals adding up to a significant amount. This chart will give you a good reality check on what you actually spend on a daily and month basis. Do this chart every month for a minimum of 1 year so you can see how your expenses fluctuate with the seasons, especially around months with holidays and during the summer. Use the results to help you plan your future budgeting and to give you ideas on which spending habits can be cut out.

DAILY EXPENSE RECORD

DATE	PURCHASES (STORE/COMPANY + ITEMS BOUGHT)	AMOUNT SPENT	CATEGORY (e.g., Entertainment, Bills, Food Out)

Money Planning Activity #3: EXPENSE SUBTRACTING LOG

Use this log to budget your money by assigning the maximum you will spend on each category per month. Write the amount you will allot to each category on the line. Keep your list handy. Whenever you purchase something in that category, subtract it from your allotted amount, and record the balance. When you make another purchase from that category, subtract the amount from the previous balance to get a new balance. Keep going for the month, but as soon as you reach $0, you are done for the month and have to wait until next month to be able to spend from that category again.

EXPENSE SUBTRACTING LOGS

$_____ - **ENTERTAINMENT**	$_____ - **TRANSPORTATION**

$_____ -	$_____ -
FOOD/GROCERIES	**PERSONAL CARE**

$_____ -	$_____ -
SHOPPING	**OTHER/GIFTS**

Add Your Own Categories:

$_____ -	$_____ -
_____	_____

PLAN YOUR HEALTH AND WELLNESS

Plan Your Health and Wellness

In order to accomplish and enjoy any of the goals, businesses, projects, and any other life desires that you want to achieve, you need to be healthy and full of energy to do so.

Therefore, it is important to plan and schedule what you will do to maintain your physical and spiritual wellness so that you can cultivate the energy and creativity required to be productive in any area of your life. Wellness is the overall feeling of wellbeing you get when you consciously give your mind, body, and spirit the attention needed in order to cultivate a balanced life.

Taking the necessary actions to care for your mind, body, and spirit automatically improves the quality of life you live and increases your ability to focus on what matters most to you, such as working on your projects and businesses, taking care of your family, and pursuing your passions.

TO CARE FOR YOUR MIND

Some activities that help to maintain positive and motivational streams into your life are reading uplifting, positive books and watching uplifting or educational videos by motivating speakers to constantly guide you toward living a positive and productive lifestyle with the purpose of being better able to accomplish your goals. See our recommended reading list in the appendix at the back of this book for suggestions to get you started.

Uplifting/Motivational/Educational Books to Read

DATE TO START READING BY	TITLE	NOTES

Purposeful Events, Workshops, Seminars, and Webinars to Attend

DATE & TIME	EVENT + DETAILS	COST	MY PURPOSE FOR ATTENDING

TO CARE FOR YOUR BODY

Living a balanced, healthy, positive lifestyle has so many proven benefits, such as overcoming physical, mental, and emotion-related illnesses and diseases and increasing your self-esteem and self-confidence. It is difficult to improve any area of your life when your physical health is less than adequate, so make it a priority to care for your physical body by incorporating regular exercise and healthy eating into your daily routine.

Write what you will do starting this month to increase or maintain a healthy physical lifestyle, and then schedule it in the chart:

_____

_____

_____

_____

_____

Physical Activity Log

DATE	ACTIVITY + LOCATION	FOR HOW LONG	CHECK

HEALTHY FOOD PLAN

Do research to find new and healthy foods you can introduce into your diet, and research the health benefits of recommended healthy foods. Make a list of the healthy foods you will incorporate into your daily routine:

Breakfast: _____

_____

_____

Lunch: _____

_____

_____

Dinner: _____

_____

_____

Snacks: _____

_____

_____

TO CARE FOR YOUR SPIRIT

You can care for your spirit in different ways, such as through prayer or meditation. When you know who you are and the reason you are on this earth, you gain a confidence and joy that enables you to face any circumstance life may bring your way. When you live with joy in your life, you have a positive outlook at all times, knowing that everything happens for a reason and that everything is a part of a greater purpose. Living with joy also means you have decided in advance to be at peace with yourself and whatever life situation may occur, and no person or thing can take that away from you.

You maintain your spiritual health by practicing the things that cultivate a positive life and only letting into your mind and spirit what you want to be there, such as love, joy, peace, patience, and forgiveness. Being quick to forgive others of their wrongdoings is an important part of your overall wellness because carrying hate and unforgiveness inside you is more harmful to your own body and mind than the person or situation you have negative feelings toward. Letting it go and practicing forgiveness sets your own self free and lifts the burden off you. When you know who you are and live in love and joy, no negative circumstances can take control of your life.

Write what you will do starting this month to increase or maintain a healthy spiritual lifestyle, and then schedule it in the chart:

_____

_____

_____

_____

_____

Spiritual Activity Log

DATE	ACTIVITY + LOCATION	FOR HOW LONG	CHECK

HOW YOUR HEALTH AND WELLNESS AFFECTS YOUR RELATIONSHIPS

Maintaining positive, mutually beneficial relationships with your family and friends is crucial to living a positive, enjoyable life, but you can't do that if you are burdened with a negative mental, emotional, and physical state of being. You can only express the love to others that you carry and practice within yourself, which is why having strong, wonderful relationships with others starts with having a strong, loving relationship with yourself. You want to maintain a strong circle of family and friends because they help to lift you up and keep you going when life gets tough and you have life challenges to overcome.

The encouragement, company, and advice from close friends and family can save your life from taking drastically wrong turns, such as preventing or helping you through depression or anxiety. Take action to maintain and improve yourself so you can continue to grow and strengthen great relationships with your family and friends.

Family and Friend Events or Meet-ups

DATE	EVENT/ MEET-UP	POSITIVE AFFIRMATIONS TO SHARE	CHECK

May You Achieve All Your Goals and Dreams.
Keep Pressing On.
Never Give Up.
You Can Do Anything You Set Your Mind To.
If You Can Dream It, You Can Achieve It!
No Dream Is Too Big, and
No Goal Is Too High.

APPENDIX

RECOMMENDED READINGS BOOK LIST:

1. *The Power of Now*, Eckert Tolle
2. *New Earth*, Eckert Tolle
3. *Freedom, Power, Grace*, Deepak Chopra
4. *Think and Grow Rich*, Napoleon Hill
5. *Rich Dad, Poor Dad*, Robert Kiyosaki
6. *Conspiracy of the Rich*, Robert Kiyosaki
7. *The Moses Code*, James F. Twyman
8. *The Alchemist*, Paulo Coelho
9. *The Greatest Salesman in the World*, Og Mandino

TIPS ON HOW TO REDUCE YOUR EXPENSES:

RUNNING A HOUSEHOLD

1. Bundle your monthly services, and negotiate with service providers for better deals (internet, cable, etc.).
2. Consider eliminating your cable or satellite TV expense altogether; watch programs on the internet.
3. Make do with either a cell phone or a landline, not both.
4. Pay bills on time to avoid late fees and interest charges.

5. Avoid excessive housing accessories, decorations, and other expenses.
6. Avoid expensive furniture and electronics that you can't pay in full right away.
7. Be smart about your energy consumption – use the off-peak times.

i) Electricity

1. Control and adjust your heating and cooling systems so they are not operating more than necessary.
2. Turn off the lights in your house when not in use; use a timer to control the lights when you're away from your house for days at a time.
3. Plug all your devices into a Smart Power Strip, which reduces the energy supply from the outlet when your device is not in use.

ii) Water

1. Preserve water; don't leave the tap running unnecessarily.
2. Use your washing and drying machines at off-peak times, which are hours when other people aren't usually washing their clothes.
3. Instead of filling the sink with water, keeping the water running, or using the dishwasher every day, wash dishes in a large container.
4. Use water-saving shower and sink tap nozzles.
5. Take care when tending to your lawn – use a timer on sprinklers and a water- efficient hose.
6. Utilize swimming pool tips, such as insulating your pool, using fitted covers when not in use, and checking for leaks.

iii) Gas

Home

1. In the hot summer months, keep all the doors closed and securely sealed in order to keep the cool air in.
2. Use a fan to just cool the room you are occupying at the moment instead of an energy-consuming air conditioner to cool the entire house.
3. In the cold winter months, maintain a regular temperature on the thermostat; use blankets and wear sweaters instead of leaving your home on full heat, which uses a lot of energy to heat the entire house.
4. Use a space heater to heat just the room you are occupying.
5. Keep the curtains open during the day to let the sunshine heat the house as well.

Car

1. Save gas by only driving when you really need to.
2. Develop good driving habits – don't be an aggressive driver; be gentle on the gas and breaks. You will save gas money and future car repair expenses and even reduce the risk of accidents and the costs associated with them.

SHOPPING

Take Personal Inventory

- Before shopping in the first place, take a detailed inventory of what is stocked on your shelves and use up what you already have. There is no need to leave half-full bottles of products or packages of food in your cupboards and then going out to buy more of the same or similar products.

- Using what you already have will extend the amount of time you need to use money from your budget to restock, whether it's for food, household items, hobby supplies, or anything else.

Reuse and Recycle

- Another way to reduce expenses is to reuse and recycle. Consider using pre-owned items in good condition by acquiring them for no cost or at a very reduced price, and you will be able to save much more money than you would by purchasing items brand new at a retail store.
- Find pre-owned items by shopping at thrift stores, garage sales, Goodwill, or online through websites like Kijiji and Craigslist where you can find low- or no-cost items.
- For clothing and accessories, either decide to be creative by finding new ways to wear what you have and making your own accessories, or go to thrift stores for less expensive items. It is possible to find nice items at thrift stores, and you can tweak the items to better suit your preferences if needed.
- You can even consult friends and family for articles they are no longer using. Buying items wholesale is also less expensive than at marked-up retail stores.

General Shopping Tips

1. Shop with cash only so you can see exactly how much you spend. Only use the cash you have with you and not the seemingly endless amount that seems available when you swipe with a debit or credit card.

2. Shop with a list and stick to it. If you see something you need that is not on your list, put it on the list for next time.
3. Shop with no cart so you eliminate the ease of access of piling things into it. With no cart, you're more likely to purchase only the few items you can carry.
4. Search for coupons and shop when there are sales.
5. Switch to store brands instead of name brands; usually it's pretty much the same thing.
6. Review the items before going to the cashier to purchase them, and ask yourself the following questions:
   a) Do I really need each item at this moment?
   b) Can I use something else that I already have at home instead?
   c) Can I get it somewhere else for less?
   Put the items back on the shelf if you can answer "no" to question a) and "yes" to questions b) and c).
7. Don't shop socially, as in, just to spend time with friends, because you are more likely to end up buying things you don't need.
8. Take a well-disciplined friend or family member shopping with you to help you avoid purchasing what you don't need, or get someone else to shop for you entirely.
9. Discuss major purchase decisions with your significant other or close family member or friend; talking it out helps you to think clearly and organize your thoughts on why or if you really need to make that purchase.
10. Give yourself 24 hours before making a purchase to allow for the initial excitement of having something new to wear off.

11. Avoid items that will eventually cause other large expenses, such as printers, which will need ink refills, and high maintenance or delicate clothing that requires dry cleaning.
12. Keep the tags on the product until the last possible minute before using or wearing it, which keeps the option open as long as possible for returning it or for finding a less expensive item that you can purchase instead.
13. Bring snacks with you when you go out so you don't have to buy any snacks or meals unnecessarily.
14. Ultimately, learn to say, "no." See how your life is not negatively affected by not making that purchase.

ENTERTAINMENT & OTHER

1. Find no-cost or inexpensive forms of entertainment, such as picnics, nature walks, community events, and arts and crafts fairs.
2. Find and use coupons for restaurants and other activities.
3. Go to events or restaurants at times of day when certain age groups or genders are free or discounted.
4. If you must eat a meal out, eat lunch out instead of dinner because lunch hour meals are generally less expensive, and you still get to enjoy the "meal out" experience and the company you are sharing it with.
5. Be aware of spending too much on new technological devices; only upgrade your devices when you really need to, and save and budget for them in advance.
6. Exercise at home or outside instead of paying for monthly gym memberships.
7. Carefully monitor your spending at holidays; don't go overboard on gift or decoration purchases.

TIPS ON CREATING EXTRA INCOME:

- As well as decreasing your expenses, be creative in coming up with ideas for ways in which you can make some extra money. Consider the following strategies:

  1. If you're a musician, you can entertain and sell your CDs at cafés, weddings, birthday parties, special events, parks, farmers' markets, and other community events.

  2. If you're a visual artist, you can offer to make commissioned orders of artwork, display at cafés, or sell your work at arts and crafts fairs and other community events.

  3. You could do odd jobs like babysitting, yard work, and house care, such as cleaning, painting, and repairing. You can also offer services for activities you're good at, like cooking, event planning, repairing, or any number of things.

  4. Sell things you don't need or no longer use, such as collectibles, items of high value, household products or supplies, furniture, clothes, jewelry, and electronics. You can hold a garage sale or use websites to sell your items online through eBay, Kijiji, or Craigslist. Go through all your possessions in all the rooms of your house and in your storage. If you find something you can make do without or haven't used in six months to one year or more, consider the fact that you may never miss it if it's gone, and therefore try to make some money from it by putting it up for sale.

  5. See if there are junk yards in your area that will pay you for dropping off scrap metal or other materials. Collect and return glass bottles to companies that pay you for returning them.

6. Before using or opening any product you purchase, ask yourself if you really, really need it or if you can make do without it. Consider returning the item with the receipt, unused and unopened, for a refund. Even if you can only get store credit for it, you can use the store credit for a time when you actually need something from that store.

7. Rent out rooms in your house to tenants, especially if you have extra guest rooms, a finished basement, or empty bedrooms due to children who have already grown up and moved away.

8. If you have a driveway and live near public transportation, popular work places, or attractions, renting out your driveway is a good way to make some quick cash. If you rent your driveway for less than a commercial parking lot, you will be providing a service that is in demand and will greatly meet people's needs.

TIPS ON HOW TO PLAN YOUR TAXES FOR YOUR BENEFIT:

TAX PLANNING STRATEGIES
By Eric Saumure, CPA, CA, President of Bytown Living

Overview

Tax planning strategies are, too often, overlooked because individuals see taxes as a necessity of doing business, for which strategies will have little to no impact after considering the high fees of accountants.

Tax planning strategies are a long-term plan, and you do not typically see significant savings in the first year. What if you could pay ½ the tax you normally would? (You could accomplish this through the use of capital gains). What if you could defer your taxes until retirement and allow your money to grow tax free? (You could accomplish this through the use of a holding corporation). What if you could pay $0 in taxes on dividends? (You could accomplish this through the use of capital dividends).

Deductions are more of an "after-the-fact" situation. It can be compared to playing hockey, and trying to make a major impact in the last half of the 3rd period. An H&R Block employee can make sure you grab all the deductions you're entitled to, but it takes a true professional to help you navigate the Income Tax Act to your optimal advantage.

Corporate Taxes

The main tax planning methodologies of corporate taxes revolve around deferring and income splitting. Many businesses pay tax at the small business rate (~16%) and then pay personal taxes when paid to individuals. The advantage from tax deferral comes from earning income in your corporation, which you don't distribute to yourself personally. This means that your cash inside your corporation will grow much faster if you only pay ~16% tax every year, instead of your personal tax rate that can be 45% or more, in Canada. Many expenses that you incur can in fact be deducted against your business income (meals with clients, home office expenses, vehicle expenses, etc.).

Income splitting is achieved by distributing your corporation's income to your spouse, children (18+ years old), or other family members. Given the tax rate for your children, spouse, or family members may be less than your tax rate, this allows you to distribute the income at an overall lower average tax rate.

Personal Taxes

Personal tax planning has slightly less creative maneuvers that can be done to help save on taxes. Nonetheless, these should not be overlooked:

TFSA – This allows you not to pay taxes on your investment income. Pure and simple.

RRSP/RESP/RDSP – These plans allow you to deduct, in the current year, your contributions to the investment plan. This enables you to typically get a refund on your taxes and use that amount to re-contribute to the plan, which effectively increases your investment anywhere from 15%-45% in one year, depending on your tax bracket. You do, however, need to pay these taxes when you take the money back out upon retiring.

Family Trusts – These can be used to split your investment income or business income, without the use of (or in combination with) a corporation. You can essentially split your income with your spouse, children, or anyone you want to. This allows you to lower the overall average tax rate.

This section is designed for you to see the potential that proper tax planning can do for you and your family's wealth. It is recommended that you contact your tax accountant for more details and specific steps that can be taken. Set yourself a goal to meet with three tax accountants and three investment advisors. Most of the time, accountant or investment advisors won't charge you for the initial consultation. Interview them! See which one you get along with the best. Ask them tough questions, and see if they deserve to be on your team.

***

WHAT EVERY SUCCESSFUL REAL ESTATE INVESTOR NEEDS TO KNOW ABOUT REAL ESTATE INVESTING

By Bruce M Firestone, PhD, Real Estate Investment coach, Century 21 Explorer Realty Inc. broker, Ottawa Senators founder, @profbruce brucemfirestone.com

Introduction: About Equity Lords

The number of mega wealthy people on this planet (a class that includes billionaires and millionaires; the latter, however, must have a net worth greater than $30 million USD to be included) is a tiny percentage of overall population—just 0.004% of adults qualify according to Wealth-X.

This group controls 12% of the world's wealth, and it keeps growing.

How did they get to be so wealthy, and, once there, how do they stay that way?

A few years ago, I did some research on the 100 wealthiest families in Canada. It might surprise you (then again, it might not) to discover that 61 out of 100, almost two thirds, had all or substantially all of their wealth in real estate. It seems that real estate is foundational—one way to both preserve and enhance multi-generational wealth.

The 6th Duke of Westminster passed away recently (August 9th, 2016) at the relatively young age of 64 but not from a lack of resources—he had to make do with/get by on a net profit from his real estate holdings (Grosvenor Group) of $14,600 USD per hour or about $128 million per year as of 2012.

The 7th Duke is now 25-years old, sole heir Hugh Richard Louis Grosvenor, deemed the United Kingdom's most eligible bachelor, not only because he's a nice looking young man but because his pocketbook also makes him attractive.

Hughie is worth about £9.35 billion (~$13 billion USD).

He's in a class of *rentiers*, an old fashioned word meaning: "a person living on income from property." Sounds like a good gig. So how do we sign up?

Well, first of all, how did Hughie get to be where he is today, other than the obvious answer: he chose the right parents?

You have to go back to 1740, the year when the great frost nearly froze everyone in Great Britain. It was the coldest year for which reliable records are available. The tune *Rule Britannia, Britannia Rules the Waves* was sung for the first time, and Sir Robert Grosvenor, 3rd Baronet, age 20, married heiress Mary Davies, age 12. He had the title; she'd inherited 500 acres north of the Thames in London where ultra-chic Belgravia and Mayfair are today.

Pretty soon thereafter, Sir Robert began development of mixed use Grosvenor Estate, made up of flats, shops, offices, and beautiful public squares.

Sir Robert also hired Warren Buffett as his financial adviser. Mr. Buffett's advice was to build and *hold*, much as Warren did centuries later with Berkshire Hathaway.

OK, OK, Warren isn't that old, so maybe he wasn't around in 1740 to give the Grosvenors any advice. In fact, it might have been the other way around.

It wouldn't surprise me to find out that Mr. Buffett studied what old European families did to become so wealthy.

In any event, Warren is worth an estimated $65.3 billion USD, so his methodology is working.

How would you apply his methodology to real estate?

1. buy or build smart
2. in great locations

3. hold onto your property
4. add value/differentiate it
5. manage it properly
6. be patient
7. refinance it every once in a while and pull out cash, tax free
8. repeat
9. pass it on to your heirs in a tax efficient and cost effective manner

I'd add a few other things like: keep your costs down, live within your means, focus on one or two types of real estate in one or two places, only buy or build property that cashflows from day one, and have as few partners as possible, the optimal number probably being zero.

The other thing would be this: want to know the fastest way to get poor? Get a divorce. So stay married if at all possible.

Lastly, there is a big hurdle for ordinary folks like you and me to get over, and, frankly, I'm not 100% sure how to do that.

Rich folks have access to very low cost debt, very. Some of the largest investors on the planet are issuing bonds that have *negative* interest rates. Investors can be people like successive Dukes of Westminster or large pension funds, REITs, publicly traded firms, insurance companies, and investment banks.

In July 2016, Bloomberg reported that Blackstone Group LP had amassed a rental portfolio in the US of more than 50,000 homes. That's *fifty thousand*. How long did that take them? Four years. I repeat: *four* years.

How long would that take you and me if we were able to buy one, say, every 2nd year? The answer is easy—*twenty-five thousand* years, and, frankly, even Warren Buffett isn't going to live that long.

What does Blackstone have that you and I don't have? Access to low cost and, possibly, negative cost debt.

CBC news reported that Canucks are also getting into the game—CIBC sold 1.25 billion Euros worth of debt with a negative yield in July 2016. Amazing.

So as a real estate investor, how quickly could you amass a top performing real estate portfolio if I lent you 1.25 billion Euros at a negative interest rate with loan to value ratios of 100% (or possibly more than 100%)?

Mighty fast, I'd be willing to guess.

What's slowing us down is the fact that lenders in Canada won't lend you more than 80% loan to value on most property. They limit you to just four or five rental properties. They certainly aren't giving you negative interest rates.

So basically, the top 0.004% of the world's population and their friends on Wall Street, Bay Street, in the City of London, Shanghai, Mumbai, Frankfurt and other major financial centers have crossed over to become equity lords and drawn up the drawbridge behind them. They've posted signs saying: KEEP OUT or NO TRESPASSING.

"Equity lord" is Neal Stephenson's term for wealthy capitalists; he uses it in his work *The Diamond Age: Or, A Young Lady's Illustrated Primer*, Bantam Dell, February 1995.

So what should ordinary real estate investors do?

Give up, right?

No way!

You have to be nimbler and cleverer, move faster, and invest in sectors where the big guys don't play.

Here's what entrepreneurs do: they do for one dollar what any other fool could do for two. They also know how to make two dollars for every dollar any fool could make.

How to Buy Residential Rental Property, Smart—Don't Be Lazy

Here are a few tips for readers who are thinking about acquiring some residential rental property to consider before they do.

"Nothing will work unless you do," Maya Angelou

a) **Get a property manager** who carefully vets tenants. You are far better off to leave the place vacant than to rent to a bad tenant. If you do have a poor tenant, an experienced property manager will know how to navigate the process to evict them.

b) **Don't ever buy a property that doesn't cashflow**. The idea that you can make up for monthly cashflow deficiencies by capital appreciation is flawed. It will crater your IRR, Internal Rate of Return.

c) **Buy low/sell high.** You make money in real estate when you buy, not when you sell. So if you get in a competitive situation and get carried away and pay too much for that cool triplex or duplex, you're sunk.

d) **Try to use all the leverage you can**—financial institutions in many nations will still lend to people with good credit (i.e., decent Beacon Scores) with just 5% or 10% down. So rather than buy one residential unit with 25% down, you could buy five of them with 5% down on each or two of them with 12.5% down. Using more leverage now will eventually allow you faster de-leveraging later assuming all your properties cashflow.

e) **If you own five units and one becomes vacant**, your vacancy rate has jumped from 0 to 20%, but if you only own one unit and it becomes vacant, your vacancy rate has leapt from 0 to 100%, which is bad.

f) **By using lots of leverage, you actually will have way more cashflow** and more forced savings and more wealth effects provided you live in a stable economic environment (like, say, Ottawa and not Arizona, Nevada, or California) and provided you followed my earlier rule—buy low.

g) **You or your property manager should visit** each of your rentals once per month. Tell your tenants in advance (some jurisdictions require you do this in writing) that you will visit once per month to collect rent personally, to inspect the unit every time you visit and to fix any problems immediately. Don't be lazy; do it. If prospective tenants don't want this, no problem. They can rent somewhere else. Those friends of mine with that 5-bedroom home near a college which was rented out to students, they visited every month bringing dinner with them (kids are always hungry). They developed solid relationships with their tenants, monitored the condition of the place, never lost a single month's room rent and even helped them with homework and personal problems when warranted.

h) **When I owned a rental property in a tough neighborhood, I co-opted the locals** including teens by hosting a FREE BBQ and blocko (short for block party) every summer. I gave all the kids (some of whom were gang members, no doubt) free burgers and flying discs and told them if they needed anything to let me know. In the years I owned the place, I had zero graffiti and vandalism—the locals looked out for it, for sure. The few hundred bucks it cost were much less expensive than higher insurance premiums. (Note: you can often get a permit to close a street for a blocko from your local municipality. They're usually free. You can invite everyone in the area by the simple expedient of a flyer drop (in some neighborhoods like the one we were in, websites/mobile apps/email/facebook/twitter/linkedin/ online invitations just aren't gonna work). Free food and beverage with some music and games (we liked Ultimate Frisbee played on the street and Paddle Tennis) will definitely bring people out. But don't serve any alcohol—this leads to fistfights and opens you up to huge liability.)

i) **You can add in-home residential apartments to your principal residence and to your rentals.** If it's your principal residence, it has the useful advantage that you don't have to travel very far to keep an eye on the place plus, part of your mortgage interest (if you still have one) becomes a business expense since you are earning income from your place. In the US, mortgage interest is already tax deductible. In Canada, your principal residence will still be capital gains tax exempt as long as the apartment is contained within the original footprint of the building, i.e., in the basement or attic say. There is government support for the cost of adding in-home rental apartments in the form of CMHC grants/loans (up to $25,000), but most of the in-home apartments that I've seen added over the years make financial sense even without soft loans or grants. Also, many cities and towns have legalized them, in part, to bring them out of the gray market and, in part, to provide more affordable housing. Legalizing them has made compliance with local building codes more likely and improved the safety of these places. I lived in one of those when I was at UCSC many years ago, and one of the granny flat plans we developed is a riff on that little place, located, I still remember, at 1011 and 1/2 Seabright Avenue in Santa Cruz, Calif. If you would like to see some of our plans, let me know via @profbruce or @Quantum_Entity.

j) **If you build or buy a duplex/triplex/multiplex, make sure you sound, smell, and fire separate** your units and they comply with all building, health, fire and safety codes. If you are purchasing an existing building, make sure you have a building inspector who knows these codes and can provide you with advice and costs estimates to make your units legal. If you discover any surprises, it's best to find these out during your conditional period when you can either abandon the deal or ask for a price abatement from the seller. Fire separation is improved by adding an extra layer of drywall. If you add it so that sheet boundaries do *not* line up, you will improve not only fire protection, you will limit sound transmission and smells between units. There are lots of simple, inexpensive things that you can do that not only improve safety for your tenants, they make their lives more enjoyable. If you are careful not to vent one unit into another, for example, you automatically reduce sound, smell and fire issues...

k) **Residential real estate returns come in three pieces:** positive monthly cashflow (aka cash-on-cash return) when rental and other income (like parking or laundry revenues) exceed expenses, forced savings/wealth effects (every month you pay your mortgage, actually, where your tenant pays your mortgage for you, you end up paying a bit of the principal off) and inflation (which comes from capital appreciation—i.e., when you sell for more than you bought).

l) **Put together a really good real estate team to advise you**—experienced coach, knowledgeable residential (and later commercial) real estate broker or salesperson, thorough building inspector who can not only tell you what's wrong with a building but how to fix it and how much that might cost, deal- making lawyer, fair appraiser (who is working for you, not the lender), honest, innovative, and competent contractors/renovators, creative interior designer and home stager, landscaper, decent property manager, plugged-in mortgage broker, etc.

What to Buy?

I often get asked: what're the best properties to buy? For most folks, it won't be:
   -office buildings
   -major shopping plazas
   -land

Why?

Well, I expect demand for office buildings to grow slowly, if at all, because of competition from the home office and co-working spaces, based as they are on a booming gig economy.

The competition to acquire assets like major regional shopping centers is fierce with large predators roaming the countryside equipped with ultra-low cost (and sometimes negative cost) financing that entrepreneurs just can't match.

And land just takes too long to develop in a municipal environment that is rabidly anti-development and bogged down by a seemingly infinite series of studies and insatiable appetite for public benefits paid for by private developers.

The lowest risk portfolio and one that is within the reach of most people is: a series of residential rental holdings, often single family homes with an in-home suite or coach house in back.

I wrote to a client of mine recently, a woman in her 30s that I coach. Here are some of the things I suggested she should look for:

- -what price are you paying/remember you make money in real estate when you buy, not when you sell, so buy smart
- -what will it cost to animate/add an in-home suite with separate entrance, add a tech package, add backyard storage shed(s) or workshops, etc.
- -how close is it to existing transit
- -how close is it to major employment nodes (colleges/ hospitals/tech/gov't)
- -how walkable is it (again, how close to jobs/shopping/ learning/mass transit/health care/recreation, etc.)
- -how rentable is it
- -check out neighborhood demographics (who is your target renter)
- -neighborhood safety and desirability
- -presence (or absence) of gentrification/folks renovating/ adding to their homes/tearing down existing ones and replacing them with bigger homes or doubles
- -proportion of renters (smaller proportion of neighborhood renting is better)
- -ability to add coach house

-locate closer to downtown/not seen as suburban
-does the area support mixed use (i.e., are services available nearby, e.g., convenient store, walk-in clinic, etc.)
-is the area densifying (e.g., doubles replacing singles) and intensifying (e.g., more work from home)

Animate Your Property

Animating property means finding ways to differentiate it and increase its income too. There are many ways to raise cap rates and ROI by:

-determining highest and best use, HABU, for each property
-adding in-home suites
-adding coach houses
-adding garage offices
-adding sheds and workshops/maker space
-adding tech packages/home automation
-adding airbnb
-adding backyard games, natural gardens, fruit trees, mini forests, nature ponds
-adding micro suites
-adding additional front yard parking (using where possible grass parking mesh)
-adding differentiated value like stand-up desks, bench seating with storage, etc.
-adding more ingress/egress to the street from the building
-adding walkout basements
-adding loft beds
-deleting corridors
-making residential leases more like commercial ones (so

that tenants pay more of the costs of running a rental property; e.g., admin fee, property management fee)
-getting professional management
-selling more services to tenants like food services, events, tutoring, etc.
-virtu car
-leasing to roommates
-energy saving LED lights and green for real
-adding micro retail
-back to back freehold towns infill
-severance possibilities
-refinancing
-proper appraisals
-CMA (comparative market analysis) sample
-decks, privacy fences, front porches
-outdoor kitchens
-outdoor TV
-theming
-wall plaques identifying building
-tagline
-advertising local businesses to tenants
-home elevators
-tribal council ring
-carports
-walkway cover
-organized street tree planting
-street parties
-outdoor lighting
-target renter market
-best marketing platforms to use to get to target market

Where to Buy Property? Where to Find Undervalued Real Estate?

Each city or town is different, and real estate is a hyper local business, so hire a realtor who knows your hometown.

Here're a few rules I use in mine (Ottawa):

-within 1,200 meters (maybe as much as 2 klicks) of transit, subway, train station, schools, hospitals, colleges, malls, tech parks, government complexes, universities, big employment nodes like the old Nortel campus (now DND), the new Ottawa Hospital location (Experimental Farm), the new LRT (light rail transit), the O-train, Zibi, LeBreton Flats, South Keys...

-west of Bank Street

-west of Westboro

-Little Italy

-Crystal Beach

-Greenbank Road

-Woodroffe Avenue

-Maitland Avenue

-Merivale Road

-Fisher Avenue

-Iris Avenue

-St. Laurent Boulevard

-Albion Road

-close to South Keys

-close to O-train

-close to Hurdman Station

-Overbrook (maybe Vanier too)

-Alta Vista

-Hunt Club

-Airport Parkway
-Belfast Road
-Tremblay Road
-Avenue O
-Avenue P
-Avenue Q
-Avenue R
-Avenue S
-Avenue T
-Avenue U

What Info You Should Have on Each Property

What info should you have on hand (which today means digitized with good quality names that you can find on your backed-up computer) for each of your properties? Below is my list.

I'm sure there is more you can and should add.

By the way, most of this info you'll also need before/during/after you make a serious offer on a new property...

- geo warehouse report (land titles showing ownership history, MPAC assessment, perimeter, area, frontage, depth, plot plan, PIN #, roll #, etc.)
- enhanced report (CMA—comparative market analysis, what other properties in the area sold for)
- PAC assessments (last two years)
- property taxes (last two years)
- survey
- building plans including as-builts plus floor plans
- environmental report (mainly for commercial property)
- well potability test (rural property)
- well record (rural property)

-septic permit (rural property)

-copies of leases

-copies of equipment rental contracts (e.g., hot water tank rental agreement)

-property management agreements (manager, snow, lawn care, etc.)

-mortgage statements

-copies of all warranties (e.g., roof, HVAC, etc.)

-copy of agreement of purchase and sale

-lawyer's report on closing

-pro pictures of the property

-copy of condo declaration (if condo)

-copy of appraisal

-copy of building inspection report

-spreadsheet for financials

-occupancy certificate

-copies of all utility payments

-copy of soil test (commercial)

-copy of hydro geo report (rural property)

-copy of MLS listing for sale (or for rent)

Believe it or not, I have most of this on most of the properties I've bought and sold on my computer, backed up in two other places, plus also in the cloud.

I am a demi-god of information and look ever so smart when I produce deliveries for amazed clients/lenders/lawyers/suppliers in a matter of seconds... by searching my database, since, you see, my computer is the other ½ of my brain...

Why You Should Treat Even Your Principal Residence as If It Were a Rental

I ask the people I coach on how to be successful real estate investors to treat even their own homes as if they were rental properties.

Why?

Well, first of all, one day, they may move out and rent it. So it could become a rental property especially since I preach buy and hold, not buy and flip.

I also believe everything you own should work for you instead of the other way round—you working to buy them.

"Buying real estate is not only the best way, the quickest way, the safest way, but the only way to become wealthy," Marshall Field, department store owner

It's why I convinced my middle daughter, Mimi (I have five great kids—three girls and two boys), to buy a semi-detached home with a walkout basement last year. We converted the basement into a nice, legal one-bedroom apartment, which rents for $1,230 per month. Mimi lives upstairs in a 3-bedroom, 2 and ½ bath home with a roommate who pays her $675 a month.

So today, she lives in her own home for about a net cash cost of $400 a month, a lot less than she was paying in rent before ($1,000/month).

So here's the process:

1. determine the HABU (highest and best use) for each property you are going to purchase, even your own home
2. think about how you could animate/renovate/increase the value of your property

3. ask what will each part of its functional program (for residences, you are talking about: the main part of the home, an in-home suite, a coach house, a workshop, a storage shed, a garage office, etc.) rent for
4. build a spreadsheet valuing the property three ways—a) on a cost to complete basis less depreciation, b) on an income basis based on actual and FMV cap rates, and c) on the basis of comparables
5. figure out what your IRR, Internal Rate of Return, is
6. share this spreadsheet with your appraiser so you can support higher valuations and improve your chances of getting decent financing and refinancing
7. make sure your head (the analytical part of you), your heart (whether you are passionate about the place), and gut (your instincts) are all in alignment; if so, this is probably a good decision

"Don't wait to buy real estate. Buy real estate and wait," Will Rogers, actor

8. then buy the place, and live happily ever after...

If you have time, please listen to what *Rich Dad, Poor Dad* author Robert Kiyosaki says in his video, *60 Minutes to Getting Rich*. While I don't agree with everything Robert says, he'll certainly convince you (I hope) that investors beat savers each and every time and that there *is* such a thing as good debt (as well as bad).

I love his definition of an asset: an asset is anything that produces cashflow (via passive income) for you even after you stop working at your JOB. A liability, on the other hand, is something that sucks money out of your jeans, whether you are working or not.

So, according to Robert, your principal home is, of course, a liability... in his world view. Naturally, if you animate it the way I've described above, it'll become an asset as well as a storehouse of value (which happens because you are "forced" to save by paying down your home mortgage).

"Every person who invests in well-selected real estate in a growing section of a prosperous community adopts the surest and safest method of becoming independent, for real estate is the basis of wealth," Theodore Roosevelt, US president

I encourage people to buy a principal residence that performs double duty. Obviously, this rules out buying homes that are vast suburban ornaments—those clearly are money suckers, not investments. That's also called "over investment."

Don't let that be you.

I think people have misunderstood some of Robert's messaging, particularly around "no money down" deal making. I actually think he's referring to self-capitalization of real estate deals via such methods as seller take back mortgages or resorting to credit cards (!) for downpayment.

And he's not talking about flipping properties either. He has a (mostly) build and hold philosophy, which I agree with.

I would also de-emphasize alternative investments like 401(k) plans in the US or RRSPs in Canada or mutual funds and insurance since many of us have experienced significant disappointment with those types of "investments."

"Now, one thing I tell everyone is learn about real estate. Repeat after me: real estate provides the highest returns, the

greatest values and the least risk," Armstrong Williams, political talk show host

The other thing I would add to Robert's teachings is how to manage property properly (a core competency) and how to add value and differentiation to your real estate (via some of the animation techniques I teach, of course!)

One other thing I like from Robert's *Rich Dad, Poor Dad* thing is that he recommends that you should retire on *debt,* not savings. This counter intuitive concept actually makes sense, I believe.

If you're not going to put money in real estate, where else?" Tamir Sapir, Manhattan real estate investor

If you save, say, $100,000 and get 1 or 2 points from your bank, that nets you $1,000 or maybe $2,000 in income per year. If, on the other hand, you borrow $100,000 to buy another income property, and it gets you a cap rate of say 6% plus some inflation protection plus some paydown of your mortgage by your tenants, you probably will see an IRR (Internal Rate of Return) of more than 24% p.a.

So skill testing question: what's better—1- or 2% ROI or 24%?

Why Invest in Real Estate?

I tell most of my SMEE (Small and Medium Sized Enterprise) clients (and my students) that real estate investing is usually a good idea. Homeownership and owning your own business premises makes sense to me in most cases. Why is that?

Well, here are a few of my reasons:

1. Forced savings—most people are really bad at saving, so, if at a minimum they own their own home or condo or (for entrepreneurs) their own business premises, every month that they make their mortgage payments, they are paying off ("saving") some of the principal. This is a type of "wealth effect"—it creates equity on your personal balance sheet (which everyone should have) or your corporate balance sheet. It is kind of a hidden part of your ROE (Return on Equity) too. Even people who are pretty good at saving their money may eventually succumb to the temptation to spend their savings. However, if their savings are tied up in bricks and mortar, they are going to have to do more than turn on their PCs and use internet banking to, say, buy that holiday of their dreams. Getting at your real estate equity can be relatively straightforward using something like a home equity Line of Credit or re-mortgaging your house, condo, or office building (or putting a "reverse" mortgage in place, something an elder might do, for example, if they are real estate "rich" but cash poor) but, at least, it requires some effort and will give you time to reflect on whether this is really what you should be doing.

2. Get rich slow—real estate is not a get rich quick scheme. But most markets have some real estate inflation and, at least, real estate markets don't usually sink as fast as say tech stocks did in the great bubble burst of the early 2000s. So if general real estate inflation is at .75% per annum, and you have 25% equity in the deal, then you are adding an extra 3% p.a. to your ROE. Obviously,

if general real estate inflation is higher than this, and it often is, this factor will play an even larger part in creating investor wealth.

3. If you own your own business premises, you have a diversification of risk. (I advise SMEEs that they should generally keep their real estate in a company separate from their operating company so that if something happens to the operating business, they can always sell their real estate holdings and, hopefully, live to fight another day).

One of my tech clients needed more and better office space. We looked at leasing 15,000 square feet of Class A office space for his cluster of companies. At that time in Ottawa, prime office space was leasing for $18 per square foot per annum triple net (that means that the tenant must pay all operating costs in addition to basic rent). Operating costs including realty taxes were in the order of $12 per square foot per annum, so 15,000 square feet of space would have cost his company in the order of $450,000 per year.

After Bill (not his real name) recovered from sticker shock, I convinced him to buy his own building. He bought a beautiful two storey, 15,000 square foot, Class A office building for $100 per square foot. He put down $500,000 and got a Vendor Take Back Mortgage (known as a VTB—i.e., his financing came from the vendor, not a bank) for the balance. His annual mortgage costs were in the order of $85,000 per annum, and he took ownership of the building in a separate company. I also convinced him to buy a house (he was renting up to that point) and to pay down both mortgages as fast as he could. Now, a few years later, Bill owns a beautiful

$750,000 home and an office building worth nearly $2m with almost no debt against them (and soon to be zero). So even if his tech company somehow goes away (which I doubt—these are very profitable enterprises), Bill can always sell his real estate for $2.75m and not eat cat food when he turns 65.

In many enterprises and especially technology and consulting companies, your key assets tend to walk out the door every night on their way home. Or in a fast changing global economy, your technology or key competitive advantage can become obsolete almost (and sometimes) overnight. Real estate doesn't usually go out of fashion as quickly*. If you look at some of the longest lasting fortunes on the planet, they tend to be (at their core) real estate based—like the House of Windsor, Emperor of Japan, Hudson's Bay Company, the old Canadian Pacific Railroad Company or the Holy Roman Catholic Church.

(*I remember a time in the 1980s when my dad got involved with a group who wanted to build Roller Disco emporiums and, boy, did they ever. I'll never forget the principal behind these developments telling me that Roller Disco (places where kids could boogie to disco music while on roller skates; they went round and round in a counter clockwise direction with lights flashing all over the place) was a "cash cow." Hey, when the kids got bored, they stopped the music, and then they went clockwise for a while. I wanted to bail out of the operating company faster than if I were a paying passenger on the Titanic. However, we managed to exchange our interest in the operating business for the underlying real estate—the Roller Disco operating entity went broke less than two years later, and we turned the real estate into a cool office for a new high tech company specializing in CAD systems which were just new at the time. Real estate has legs; Roller Disco was just a fad.)

4. If you own rental property, your tenants are helping you with your "forced savings" since they are paying off the part of the principal on your mortgage every month for you.

Buildings Don't Tend to Run out on You

5. Hopefully, your real estate portfolio is providing you with some cash-on-cash return too so that every month you are getting some help with what my spouse, Dawn, calls "IGA money," after the IGA grocery store that she used to frequent; i.e., money you can touch, feel, and *spend.*

6. You will have security of tenure since the landlord (yourself) won't raise your rent every five years or so, especially if you are doing well financially. There seems to be a rule in life that costs always rise to whatever your income is. This is as true for a company as it is for an individual; Landlords just have a sixth sense about these things and can keep on increasing your rent until you simply have to move.

7. Brand equity—you do develop a kind of brand equity in your location over time, and if you own the real estate, at least you are developing brand equity in your own property, not someone else's.

8. Brand equity is important because it helps you build up your credibility; credibility and trust are hugely

important in sales—people like to buy from people they like and trust. The two things often go together. Did you ever buy from someone you didn't like and didn't trust—not too often, I'll bet?

That's why mega corporations spend so much money building their brand; it's so that when one of their salespeople is in the trenches competing for a sale and trying to close the deal, they often get the nod over the competition because they are a known (read *trusted*) commodity. Imagine if you were hearing an insurance pitch from somebody who worked for the Pirate Insurance Company of Kinakua versus somebody who worked for Clarica. Which one would you be more likely to put your trust in and trust your family's future to?

Companies spend money on marketing their brand not just so you can watch the Super Bowl on free TV—they spend money on ads so they can *increase sales* but not in the way most people think of it. By spending $$$ on TV ads to establish a new brand (like Clarica did in 2002 and 2003), they don't actually expect 100,000 people to suddenly call their call center and order life insurance. They know better than that.

They understand that all the marketing in the world doesn't sell much, if anything—they need a *separate process* to harvest the goodwill that they have generated in their marketing blitz. All that their marketing has done is increase the propensity-to-buy. The separate sales process involves a huge team of focused, Clarica salespeople—the sales team is like the "facts on the ground" in military/political speak. They are in the trenches with consumers selling one customer at a time. Each in-the-trenches sales team member has a greater *likelihood* of making the sale because of the mass marketing that Clarica has done, but that is all that marketing dollars can do—increase the probability of a sale and only if there is actual selling activity going on.

9. Owning your own location instantly builds credibility with suppliers, bankers, employees and others whom you depend on too.

10. If you want to make any changes to the premises, you can without investing your money in someone else's building or having to ask permission.

11. Once you have paid off your mortgage, you can either continue to have the operating company pay rent and enjoy another income stream, or you can benefit from "tax-free, unearned" rent. The latter is another type of wealth effect* (which is also why you want to pay off your home mortgage as fast as you can pretty much everywhere in the world today except perhaps the USA where mortgage interest on your personal home is tax deductible, which changes the calculations a bit).

(*This wealth effect is also quite real. Suppose you own your own building, and the mortgage is fully paid off. Now you decide to reduce your rent to zero. Your operating company's net income goes up by an amount equal to the rent they paid in the last year of the mortgage, an amount equal to Y dollars. Now in Canada, related inter-company dividends are tax free, so you could dividend out the equivalent amount to your real estate holding company. Whereas before you had income in the holding company (of course, you had some offsetting expenses too), now you have inter-company, tax-free dividends.

For your personal home, it works a bit differently. Let's

say you have a home worth $300,000, and you have finished paying off the mortgage. And let's say you could rent it out for $3,000 a month. If your marginal tax bracket is 50%, then you are left with $18k after tax, less whatever costs you might have against this. But if you stay in the home, you are enjoying the benefit of living there on "unearned rent" (a British term) of $36k a year—which isn't taxed. Unearned rent is also sometimes referred to as "imputed rent."

Another way of looking at it is if you moved out of the home, rented it for $3k a month and rented another exactly equivalent house for yourself (you have to live somewhere after all) at $3k a month, you are gaining $18k in after tax income but paying $36k in after tax rent yourself, so you end up actually *losing* $18k on the whole deal. It's weird but true—people who have paid off their home mortgages may not understand the exact mechanics of this wealth effect, but they sure feel it. They tell me things like: "I seem to have more money than I ever did when I was working. I just seem to have more cash around these days..."

"Unearned" rent is a concept that originally seems to have derived from a British sensibility that owners of real property are somehow undeserving of a return on capital. No doubt this is a class-based concern. There have been attempts to tax homeowners who have no mortgages on their residences on their "unearned" rents—one attempt in Switzerland and one in Australia that I know about. Both were roundly hated by the populace and were rescinded shortly after introduction in Switzerland and never actually implemented in Australia.

One also has to think that taxing unearned rents would work against thriftiness on the part of homeowners and against social order too. Evidence abounds that people who own their own homes tend to see themselves as having more of a stake in their societies—they tend to vote in civic elections, participate in volunteerism and form the bedrock of a civil society.

In addition, home equity and real estate equity more generally are the bedrock source of friendly capital for startups. The work of Hernando De Soto in LDCs (least developed countries) has shown that until they: a) recognize private property rights, b) give clear legal title in (and civic addresses to) real property to sitting owners and c) develop a competitive market for financing of real property (a system of mortgage financing), they cannot unlock real estate capital for redeployment to productive, entrepreneurial uses.)

12. It is often cheaper to own than to rent especially in low interest rate countries like Canada and the US today.

13. You should want to own your own real estate without partners if you can swing it. There are still: 'Two chairs up in Heaven waiting for the first two partners to get there and still like each other." (Anon.) But if you do take on a partner to acquire real estate, make sure that you both have the same financial incentives and goals*. (*In a bankruptcy of one of my dad's (Jack) real estate partners, five properties jointly owned by Jack and Les (not his real name) were caught up in major court proceeding along with 75 other projects. A major, publicly traded real estate business wanted to buy all 80 properties out of bankruptcy including the halves of the five projects that Jack owned with Les.

Two things saved my dad—he had the good sense to enter into first right of refusal agreements on all five properties with Les, and he had me to negotiate with the major realty company we'll call DevCo.

DevCo was buying Les' half of each of the five properties in question for $400,000. Our internal valuation carried these projects at $2.2m, and that was just for our halves. Andy Jenkins (not his real name), V.P. for DevCo, told me that we had two choices—sell our half interests for $400,000 or stay in and become partners with DevCo. "Why not be partners with DevCo?" he said. "We are a national company with a national network of leasing and operating executives." Why not, indeed?

Our concern was that DevCo had a lot of other vacant buildings near these properties—geez, they could actually make money by taking tenants out of our buildings (where they would own 50%, and we would own 50%) and putting them in buildings that they owned 100%. After a couple of years, we might have been lucky to get an offer from DevCo for our half interests where we did not have to *pay* them for accumulated losses just to take our share off our hands. I hate 50/50 partnerships anyway. No one is in charge; no one has final say; it's a recipe for stalemate and disaster. If you are going to have partners, at least have someone own 51%, and you know where the buck stops. So we exercised our rights of refusal and offered to buy Les' halves for $400,000 (it's like a right to match). Jenkins and his boss went nuts. They told me they would "see us in court" where they would argue the "greater good" theory—that the bankruptcy judge should override our rights because the greater good (i.e., DevCo's greater good) demanded that all 80 properties be dealt with in one fell swoop.

A couple of days before the hearing, Jenkins asked me what we wanted for our half interests. I told him $2.2m, and he blanched. I argued that he was still getting a good deal—he had Les' half for $400k and ours for $2.2m for a total of $2.6m on buildings we valued at $4.4m, so he was getting them for about 50% of their value anyway. He said: "See ya in court."

Ten minutes before the hearing began, Jenkins asked again. I said, "$2.2m." We dickered for a few minutes and settled at the courthouse door for... $2.1m.

This got Terrace Investments Ltd. going—eight years later (in 1990), we acquired the Ottawa Senators franchise from the NHL for $50m; some of DevCo's money was in that deal.)

14. Owning your own real estate gives you more financial flexibility—borrowing based on real estate collateral is usually much easier than, say, using your IP to secure a loan. The financial markets are much more developed and flexible for real property (at least in North America) than for Intellectual Property. Home equity loans are generally readily available to homeowners if they have a good credit rating (and sometimes even if they don't). Home equity loans are the largest single source of capital to start your own business. They are also used by homeowners if they get into financial trouble or lose their jobs.

15. Nations that are made up of homeowners and business owners who own their own real estate are usually more robust societies where ownership of real estate conveys a sense of permanence, social responsibility, and civic pride.

Bruce Murray Firestone, B Eng (Civil), M Eng-Sci, PhD

Bruce M Firestone is best known as an entrepreneur and founder of NHL hockey team, the Ottawa Senators, their home arena, Canadian Tire Centre, and the Ottawa Senators Foundation, a children's charity, as well as author, professor, coach, consultant, mentor, real estate broker (with Century 21 Explorer Realty Inc.), columnist, novelist and urban guru. Prof Bruce is an effective keynote speaker for organizations with a positive focus on creating opportunities for their stakeholder group. Firestone also advises counties, towns, and cities as well as economic development agencies on how to develop live-work-play-learn-shop-grow-make-build-affordable-diversified-sustainable-visitable-neo-urbanist communities based on the principle that nothing is sustainable unless it is also economically sustainable.

You can follow Firestone on twitter @ProfBruce and @Quantum_Entity and read one of his blogs at www.profbruce.tumblr.com. You can find his works at www.brucemfirestone.com.

His current motto is, *"Making Impossible Possible."*

ABOUT THE AUTHORS

Prea Zwarych is best known for her creativity and supreme management, organizational, and planning skills. Prea is a passionate entrepreneur, visual artist, and author. She started managing residential real estate after she successfully teamed up with other investors to invest in and renovate properties through joint-venture agreements.

Fenol E. is a driven entrepreneur, real estate investor, and author. Through self-discipline, perseverance, and hard work, he has overcome some of the toughest circumstances in his life such as living in poverty, eating one meal a day (if lucky), and not receiving a good education growing up.

Prea started her first business, selling her paintings, at the age of 15. She graduated with Honours from the University of Ottawa with a Bachelor of Fine Art degree and a minor in Arts Administration. Prea inspires people to use their creativity, passions, and skills to better their lives and make a positive impact on the world.

Fenol launched his first business venture at the age of seven selling mangoes to survive. His real estate investing journey started after he read the book *Rich Dad, Poor Dad* by Robert Kiyosaki in 2004, which inspired him to build a company that manages and invests in real estate. Fenol's greatest passion is helping others grow and expand in business and life through sharing powerful wisdom, and lessons he has learned, and experiences he has acquired over the years.

Together, Prea and Fenol founded Makkai Real Estate Investing, Inc., a real estate investing and management company helps homeowners generate additional income with their homes and helps landlords and investors increase their cash flow and minimize vacancies through creative property management and Airbnb bookings.

Makkai Real Estate Investing, Inc.
www.makkairei.com
info@makkairei.com

Printed in the United States
By Bookmasters